T0414035

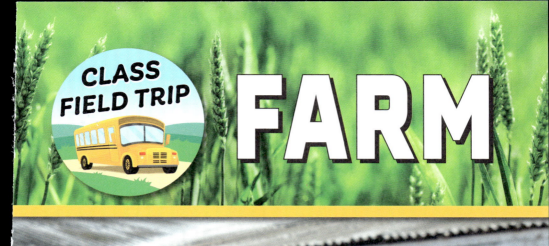

FARM
CLASS FIELD TRIP

Corinne Fickett

A Crabtree Roots Book

Crabtree Publishing
crabtreebooks.com

School-to-Home Support for Caregivers and Teachers

This book helps children grow by letting them practice reading. Here are a few guiding questions to help the reader with building his or her comprehension skills. Possible answers appear here in red.

Before Reading:
- What do I think this book is about?
    - *I think this book is about how farms work.*
    - *I think this book is about the parts of a farm.*

- What do I want to learn about this topic?
    - *I want to learn what there is to do at a farm.*
    - *I want to learn what kinds of animals you can see at a farm.*

During Reading:
- I wonder why…
    - *I wonder what pigs like to eat.*
    - *I wonder why there is a tractor at a farm.*

- What have I learned so far?
    - *I have learned that you can see goats at a farm.*
    - *I have learned that you can watch pigs eat.*

After Reading:
- What details did I learn about this topic?
    - *I have learned that you can go on a tractor ride.*
    - *I have learned that visiting a farm is fun.*

- Read the book again and look for the vocabulary words.
    - *I see the word **farm** on page 3 and the word **goats** on page 9. The other vocabulary words are found on page 14.*

We go to the **farm**.

We listen to the **farmer**.

We watch some **pigs** eat.

We pet the **goats**.

We go on a **tractor** ride.

The farm is fun!

Word List
Sight Words

a	listen	the
eat	on	to
fun	pet	watch
go	ride	we
is	some	

Words to Know

farm

farmer

goats

pigs

tractor

29 Words

We go to the **farm**.

We listen to the **farmer**.

We watch some **pigs** eat.

We pet the **goats**.

We go on a **tractor** ride.

The farm is fun!

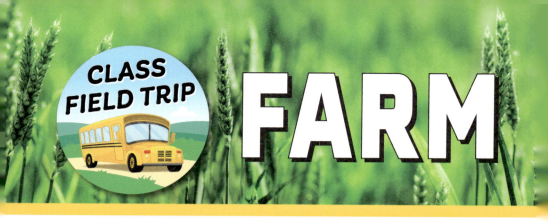

Written by: Corinne Fickett
Designed by: Bobbie Houser
Series Development: James Earley
Proofreader: Melissa Boyce
Educational Consultant: Marie Lemke M.Ed.

Photographs:
Shutterstock: HappyPictures: cover logo, p. 16; Lena Platonova: cover; Jenoche: p. 1; Jon Bilous: p. 3, 14; Kikujiarm: p. 4, 14; Irina Papoyan: p. 7, 14; Sandra Lorenzen-Mueller: p. 8, 14; The Image Party: p. 10-11, 14; Stanislaw Mikulski: p. 13

Crabtree Publishing

crabtreebooks.com   800-387-7650
Copyright © 2025 Crabtree Publishing
All rights reserved. No part of this publication may be reproduced, stored in a retrieval system or be transmitted in any form or by any means, electronic, mechanical, photocopying, recording, or otherwise, without the prior written permission of Crabtree Publishing.

Published in Canada
Crabtree Publishing
616 Welland Ave.
St. Catharines, Ontario
L2M 5V6

Published in the United States
Crabtree Publishing
347 Fifth Ave
Suite 1402-145
New York, NY 10016

Library and Archives Canada Cataloguing in Publication
Available at Library and Archives Canada

Library of Congress Cataloging-in-Publication Data
Available at the Library of Congress

Hardcover: 978-1-0398-4449-0
Paperback: 978-1-0398-4530-5
Ebook (pdf): 978-1-0398-4606-7
Epub: 978-1-0398-4676-0
Read-Along: 978-1-0398-4746-0
Audio: 978-1-0398-4816-0

Printed in the USA/062024/CG20240201